D1540603

HENNY YOUNGMAN'S
999 FUNNIEST ONE-LINERS

HENNY YOUNGMAN'S
999 FUNNIEST ONE-LINERS

by
HENNY YOUNGMAN

Illustrated by
Jerry Van Amerongen

WINGS BOOKS
New York • Avenel, New Jersey

This 1994 edition is published by Wings Books,
distributed by Random House Value Publishing, Inc.,
40 Engelhard Avenue,
Avenel, New Jersey 07001,
by arrangement with the author.

Random House
New York • Toronto • London • Sydney • Auckland

Printed and bound in the United States of America

Library of Congress Cataloging-in-Publication Data

Youngman, Henny.
Henny Youngman's 999 funniest one liners /
by Henny Youngman ; illustrated by Jerry Van Amerongen.
p.   cm.
ISBN 0-517-10187-4
I. Title.   II. Title: Henny Youngman's nine hundred
ninety-nine funniest one liners.
PN6162.Y594   1994
818'.5202—dc20   94-8392
                                                    CIP

8 7 6 5 4 3 2 1

CONTENTS

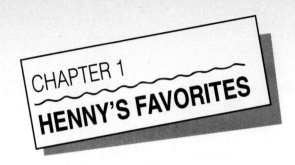

CHAPTER 1
HENNY'S FAVORITES

I looked high and low for you, I didn't look low enough.

I don't believe in reincarnation, but what were you when you were alive?

Don't move—I want to forget you just the way you are.

If they can make penicillin out of old moldy bread, surely they can make something out of you.

How can you talk all night without stopping to think?

If you had your life to live over again—do it overseas.

He was born at home but when his mother saw him she went to the hospital.

Was that suit made to order? "Yes." Where were you at the time?

You have the Midas touch. Everything you touch turns into a muffler.

If you have your life to live over again, don't do it.

 He spends money like water, drip, drip, drip.

I'd put a curse on you, but somebody beat me to it.

I know this man through thick and thick.

Four drunks looked at him, they took the pledge.

The trouble with traveling by airplane is that you can't walk out on a dull movie.

He's a real good egg, and you know where eggs come from.

I'd like to say we're glad you're here—I'd like to say it . . .

You look like a talent scout for a cemetery.

Someday you'll go too far, and I hope you'll stay there.

He's hoping for a lucky stroke—his rich uncle's.

When you get up in the morning, who puts you together?

At least he gives his wife something to live for—a divorce.

For short people: I've been looking low and low for you.

Henny's Favorites

May we have the pleasure of your absence?

What got you out of the woodwork?

I can't forget the first time I laid eyes on you—and don't think I haven't tried.

I'm going to name my first ulcer after you.

Why don't you step outside for a few years?

Why don't you go to a window and lean out too far?

I know you have to be somebody—but why do you have to be you?

I never forget a face, and in your case I'll remember both of them.

You appear to be as happy as if you were in your right mind.

It's good to see you. It means you're not behind my back.

You know, I'd like to send you a Valentine, but I haven't figured out how to wrap lace around a time bomb.

You're the kind of person I would like to have over when I have the measles.

Was the ground cold when you crawled out this morning?

I remember you—you're a graduate of the Don Rickles School of Charm.

 Who shines your suits?

Sit down; you make the place look shabby.

I'm paid to make an idiot out of myself. Why do you do it for free?

There's only one thing that keeps me from breaking you in half; I don't want two of you around.

If there's ever a price on your head, take it.

If I were you, I'd return that face to Abbey rents.

Are you naturally stupid or are you waiting for a brain transplant?

He has more crust than a pie factory.

He doesn't get ulcers, he gives them.

He should have been an undertaker—he has no use for anyone living.

Some people bring happiness wherever they go. You bring happiness whenever you go.

There's a pair of shoes with three heels.

Look at him, sex takes a holiday.

If it pays to be ignorant, why are you always broke?

Zsa Zsa Gabor has been married so many times she has rice marks on her face.

Mickey Rooney has been married so many times he has a wash and wear tuxedo.

He had a nightmare last night, he dreamed that Dolly Parton was his mother and he was a bottle baby.

Henny's Favorites

Let me tell you about our guest of honor. Never has a man been more sworn at—more spit at—more maligned—and rightfully so!

There's one good thing about being bald—it's neat.

He dresses like an unmade bed!

You're perfect for hot weather. You leave me cold.

He doesn't have an enemy in the world—he's outlived them all.

I think the world of you—and you know what condition the world is in today.

There's only one thing wrong with you. You're visible.

I understand you throw yourself into everything you undertake; please go and dig a deep well.

Why don't you sit down and rest your brains?

I'm planning to invite you to my party—there's always room for one bore.

There's a train leaving in one hour. Be under it!

I'll never forget the first time we met—but I'm trying.

He was the only man ever kicked out of the army for looking like a one-man slum.

If you'll stop telling lies about me I'll stop telling the truth about you.

I don't know what makes you tick, but I hope it's a time bomb.

Next time you give your clothes away—stay in them.

Why don't you start neglecting your appearance? Then maybe it'll go away.

I enjoy talking to you. My mind needs a rest.

It's nice hearing from you—next time send me a post card.

You have a nice personality—but not for a human being.

Look, I'm not going to engage in a battle of wits with you—I never attack anyone who is unarmed.

I'd like to introduce you to some friends of mine. I want to break off with them.

Is your family unhappy? Or do you go home at night?

I wish somebody would kidnap you—but who would they contact?

Someday you'll find yourself and will you be disappointed.

I like you—I have no taste, but I like you.

When the grim reaper comes for you he'll have a big smile on his face.

 There's a guy who lives alone and looks it.

Do me a favor—on your way home, make it a point to jaywalk.

I'd like to run into you again—sometime when you're walking and I'm driving.

Henny's Favorites

His friends don't know what to give him for Christmas. What do you give to a guy who's had everybody?

If Moses had known you, there would positively have been another Commandment.

The more I think of you the less I think of you.

He lights up a room when he leaves it.

What do you give a guy who has nothing?

Lots of people owe a lot to him—ulcers, nausea, diarrhea.

Don't sell him short. In college he was a four letter man and they called him bleep.

They change the sheets daily—from one room to another.

Henny's Favorites

I love that man—very few people know this man was born an only twin.

He was a real gentleman. He reminds me of Saint Paul—one of the dullest towns in America.

The things he does for his friends can be counted on his little finger.

You have a ready wit. Let me know when it's ready.

If you were alive, you'd be a very sick man.

The last time he was in a hospital, he got get-well cards from all the nurses.

I solved the parking problem, I bought a parked car.

I ran away from home—and my mother couldn't find me. She didn't even look.

I was so big, when I was born, the doctor was afraid to slap me.

A trombone looks better in my derby than I do.

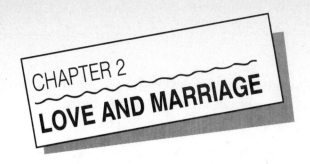

CHAPTER 2
LOVE AND MARRIAGE

Alimony is a case of wife and debt.

Alimony is the fee you have to pay for name dropping.

Alimony is repossessed love that one must still pay out on the installment plan.

It's better to have loved and lost—provided you don't have to pay alimony.

Paying alimony is like paying the installments on a wrecked car.

The biggest surprise the average husband can give his wife on their anniversary is to remember it.

When I win an argument with my wife the argument is not over.

My wife wanted a foreign convertible. I bought her a rickshaw.

Fools rush in where bachelors fear to wed.

Show me a bigamist, and I'll show you a man who believes that two beds are better than one.

Bigamy is where two rites make a wrong.

My wife is unpredictable. She doesn't want to be reminded of her birthdays, and is disappointed when I forget them.

My wife wanted a foreign convertible. I bought her a rickshaw.

Conscience makes you tell your wife—before somebody else does.

My wife could even have the last word with an echo.

 I've tried to argue with my wife, but her words flail me.

I have terrible luck—last week my chauffeur ran off without my wife.

Each time my wife goes on a diet, all she loses is her sense of humor.

My wife diets religiously—one day a week.

I lost over one hundred pounds last week—my wife left me!

They're called divorce suits because nothing but a divorce seems to suit.

She lost the marriage, but she won the divorce.

We found out we weren't fit to be tied.

It's called grounds for divorce because of the dirt.

The only way to get a doctor to make a house call is to marry him.

My wife has an ear like a shovel. Always picking up dirt.

Most marriage failures are caused by failures marrying.

My wife comes from such an old family—it's been condemned.

In my marriage, the problems are all relative.

A lot of people who wouldn't bet on a horse turn around and get married.

At the movies, they have to ask my wife to take off her hair.

My wife and I never quarrel in public—that's what we have a home for.

If my wife doesn't stop nagging me, I'll let my insurance lapse.

I don't mind my wife walking on me, but she wears spiked heels.

A girl needs a husband to share her joys, sorrows, and her friends' secrets.

I always have the last word in my marriage—it's usually "Yes."

My wife is never happier than when I'm poking funds at her.

Love and Marriage

Men would rather be the second husband of a widow than the first.

Marriage brings out the animal in some men, usually the chicken.

I'm so henpecked, I have to wash and iron my own apron.

Lover's Leap: the distance between two beds.

The quickest way to go broke is to start loving beyond your means.

Love is like a game of chess. One false move and you're mated.

Love makes the world go around looking for a divorce lawyer.

Life would be happier if love were as easy to keep as it is to make.

I worship the ground her father struck oil on.

Platonic love is like a gun that seems not to be loaded—but it always is.

Love at first sight is possible, but it always pays to take a second look.

If this isn't love, it'll have to do until I get some sleep.

All's fair in love and war and they are alike in other ways.

The hard part is to love your neighbor as your self.

Not every husband lies to his wife—some men prevaricate.

My wife hasn't been herself lately—and I hope she'll stay that way.

I don't mind my wife walking on me, but she wears spiked heels.

My wife is very quick on the flaw.

My wife can make more cutting remarks than a surgeon.

I always take bad luck like a man—I blame it on my wife.

I put a ring on her finger and she put one through my nose.

A word to my wife is never sufficient.

They didn't marry for love or money—but for a short time.

I never realized how unimportant I was until I went to my own wedding.

My wife has a sobering effect on me—she hides the bottle.

Love and Marriage

Nothing is written less about than a June bridegroom.

My wife can dish it out, but she can't cook it.

The groom is never important at a wedding unless he doesn't show up.

My wife deserves a lot of credit—but she demands cash.

Today a marriage contract is just a short term option.

Marriage is the hangover from the intoxication of passion.

Marriage is the original on-the-job training institution.

Since "Here Comes The Bride" I've constantly been facing the music.

Marriage is a knot tied by a preacher and untied by a lawyer.

Marriage is all right—it's living together afterwards that's so difficult.

I was married by a judge—I should have held out for a jury.

When two movie stars get married, their lawyers live happily ever after.

The only instrument I play is second fiddle at home.

The greatest martial music ever written is the wedding march.

When a husband is too good to be true, he probably isn't.

Try praising your wife, even if at first it frightens her.

Love and Marriage

My wife missed her nap today. She slept right through it.

My wife hasn't been feeling well. Something she agreed with is eating her.

I won't let my wife work. I'm afraid to stay home alone.

CHAPTER 3
FAMILY AND HOME

My mother-in-law is going to live to a gripe old age.

My son is a typical American teenager—he's 34.

The walls in my apartment are so thin that I recently asked a visitor a question and got three answers.

I finally figured out how to make a landlord paint your apartment—move out.

Our new baby keeps my wife from having an eight hour day, and me from having an eight hour night.

The only time my wife suffers in silence is when she's waiting for me to get up and take care of the baby.

A baby sitter is a teenage girl you hire to let your children do whatever they want.

Time is relative. How long a few minutes are depends on whether you are in the bathroom or out.

Show me a twin birth and I'll show you an infant replay.

What is a home without children? Quiet.

Show me an illegitimate child and I'll show you a sinfant.

My kid is too young to drive—so he steals taxis.

My son is very talented. At ten he's playing the piano and the horses.

Children are a great comfort in your old age—and they help you reach it.

I grew up to be the kind of kid my mother didn't want me to play with.

I was a tough kid. At six I was the chief repaint man for a hot tricycle ring.

He's a father? They must have lowered the requirements.

Outlaws may be a menace to society, but in laws are worse.

 To teach your kids the value of money—borrow from them.

They're having trouble getting a divorce—neither one wants the children.

Mom never drinks anything stronger than pop—and Pop will drink anything.

My ancestors didn't come on the Mayflower—they had their own boat.

I can trace my family tree back to when my family lived in it.

My brother-in-law is so seedy, he won't go near a canary.

A big family is proof that married folks love children—or something.

Dad's with the F.B.I.—they caught up with him in Los Angeles.

Speaking of trade relations, almost everyone would like to.

I think there's insanity in my family. They keep writing me for money.

Dad was a wonderful baseball player. I was his first error.

A close relative is one you see occasionally between family funerals.

It's a wise child who resembles a close relative.

We have a lazy susan in the middle of our living room—my sister-in-law.

Even after a man loses his last friend he still has his relatives.

My daughter gained 150 pounds last spring. She finally found a husband.

A distant relative is one who recently borrowed money from you.

Why is it that people who live the longest are rich relatives?

Adam must have been a happy man. He didn't have a mother-in-law.

Breakfast in bed is the hardest meal for a mother to get.

I broke our dog from begging for food at the table—I let him taste it.

My dad ran a farm with less equipment than I need to keep my lawn.

About all I've been able to grow in my garden is tired.

Gardening is a painstaking endeavor, especially in the small of the back.

To raise a successful garden you should use trowel and error.

The only thing I've been able to grow is round shouldered.

My brother-in-law is so seedy, he won't go near a canary.

The biggest worry of a doting father is a dating daughter.

Where do mothers learn all the things they tell their daughters not to do?

My brother-in-law has the gift of grab.

My kid makes me wish that birth control was retroactive.

My brother-in-law is a fugitive from a brain gang.

My uncle is recovering from an odd accident. An idea struck him.

My brother-in-law was in a fight once, and was knocked conscious.

You can't flout all the laws—there are the in-laws.

Man is lazy by nature so God gave us children to get us up early.

If work is a virtue, my brother-in-law is living in sin.

My brother-in-law is so lazy he won't even exercise discretion.

My brother-in-law is so lazy he's become a landmark.

My brother-in-law is so lazy that his self winding watch ran down.

My father lived to be ninety, but liquor and women finally got him.

Platonic love is possible, but only between a husband and a wife.

My sister is in the dumps, she's in love with a garbage man.

I had to propose to my wife in the garage—I couldn't back out.

Every time I find a girl that I love, my father marries her.

My father-in-law lies like an affidavit.

The only thing my mother-in-law shares willingly is a disease.

Embark on the sea of matrimony and you wind up with a raft of kids.

Anniversary: the day on which you forget to buy a present.

Adam had no mother-in-law—that's how we know he lived in paradise.

Be kind to your mother-in-law. Baby sitters are expensive.

I always tell my wife "I like your mother-in-law better than mine."

You're not really successful until your mother-in-law admits it.

 My mother-in-law's social security number is 2.

A parent believes the words "progeny" and "prodigy" are interchangeable.

Parents are what children wear out faster than their shoes.

A father is a man who is working his son's way through college.

Father's replace the cash in their wallets with photos of their kids.

Know what my son is going to be when he graduates? An old man.

~~~~~~

Children never discuss sex in the presence of their elders.

He comes from the shady side of his family tree.

My television set has only two controls: my wife and my child.

~~~~~~

CHAPTER 4
SUCCESS/MONEY/LUCK

If you don't take your lawyer's advice, do you still have to pay him?

After looking at the bill for my operation I understand why they wear masks in the operating room.

My credit is so bad, I can't even borrow trouble.

I have a sure fire way to save money. I forget who I borrowed it from.

If a fool and his money are soon parted, who got yours?

My wallet is always full of big bills—all unpaid.

Even as a boy I had to scrimp and scrape—I saved every cent I stole.

I've got two changes of clothing—with and without.

These are my summer clothes. Summer paid for and summer not.

I thought talk was cheap until I saw our telephone bill.

Money talks, and that's the conversation I'm most interested in.

Crime doesn't pay. Nice hours though.

Crime doesn't pay, unless of course, you do it well.

My credit is so bad, they won't even take my cash.

A deadbeat doesn't care whose means he lives beyond.

Give a man credit for anything today, and he'll take it.

A man who is long in debt is usually short in money.

Loan sharks attack those who go out beyond their financial depth.

 There is nothing as short as short term debt.

About the only thing a man can acquire without money is debt.

My doctor put me back on my feet. To pay his bill, I had to sell my car.

If ignorance is bliss, why aren't more people happy?

Money talks, but it's hard of hearing when you call it.

Our home is in a nice location—just on the outskirts of our income.

He thinks he's worth a lot of money just because he has it.

His trouble is that he let his father's success go to his head.

I never made Who's Who, but I'm listed in Who's Through.

I had the right aim in life, but I ran out of ammunition.

I'm money-mad. I never had any—that's why I'm mad.

My luck! The last time I turned over a new leaf, it was poison ivy.

I rose from obscurity and am now headed for oblivion.

I thought I was on the right track until I got run over sitting there.

The best way to find a missing relative is to become very rich.

I come from a wealthy family. My brother is worth $50,000.00—dead or alive.

My idea of a seven-course dinner is a hot dog and a six-pack.

Two can live as cheaply as one—if one doesn't eat.

I never forget a friend, especially if he owes me money.

I have friends I haven't even used yet.

One sure way to learn how to pray is to play poker.

In poker it's darkest just before you've drawn.

I'm really unlucky. In Las Vegas, I even lost $10.00 on the stamp machine.

I gambled away the rent money. It was a moving experience.

One thing I've discovered is that trees grow on money.

Golf isn't a rich man's game—there are plenty of poor players.

I almost made a hole-in-one today—I just missed by three strokes.

While it pays to be honest, it's often a long time collecting.

I'd be willing to earn my money honestly if it didn't take so long.

I once crossed a horse with a fish. I put a fin on its nose.

No horse can go as fast as the money you bet on him.

The horse I bet on was so slow he was arrested for loitering.

I had a good day at the races. I didn't go.

It is possible to win money at the race track—if you're a fast horse.

I always do the right thing too late, or the wrong thing too soon.

You're famous when a crazy person imagines that he is you.

I made so much hush money, I had to whisper my bank deposits.

I'm in the upper brackets. I stole $100,000.00 from my last employer.

A man is known by the company he keeps—getting dividends from.

In the stock market a dividend is a certain per cent, per annum, perhaps.

Another very annoying place to live is just beyond your income.

What used to cost $5.00 to buy, now costs $25.00 to fix.

When money talks, all too often it says "Not Guilty."

The man who said talk is cheap, never hired a lawyer.

I found a great way to start the day—I go back to bed.

If I inherited a pumpkin farm, they'd outlaw Halloween.

I seem to go through life pushing doors marked "Pull."

Ten years ago I was an unknown failure—now I'm a known failure.

To save money at the movies, we buy one ticket and take turns.

Money can't buy love, but it can put you in a better bargaining position.

Money can't buy love, but it makes shopping for it a lot easier.

Luck explains the success of people you don't like.

Miss Fortune visits me more often than Lady Luck.

A rabbit's foot may be lucky; but the original owner wasn't.

Anyone who has the time to look for a four leaf clover really needs to find one.

Lady Luck smiles on a few of us, but laughs at the rest of us.

Many men are not superstitious because they think it brings bad luck.

If I didn't have bad luck I wouldn't have any luck at all.

Talk about bad luck! I opened a fortune cookie and found a summons.

Never tell a lie when the truth is more profitable.

I'm the kind of guy who gets sick on his day off.

I was too poor to get married, but I found it out too late.

I went bankrupt three times and didn't make a cent once.

If it weren't for the misfortune of others, life would be unbearable.

A sign saying "Jesus Saves." Underneath it somebody wrote "Moses Invests."

Am I rich? Why my bank account is named after me.

You can't take it with you, but where on earth can you go without it?

I just read a book with nothing in it: my bankbook.

I always take my salary to the bank. It's too small to go by itself.

Rome isn't the world's most beloved capital—money is.

The only thing you can get without money is sick.

Money is not the root of all evil—no money is.

The hardest thing to get hold of these days is easy money.

My paycheck is like the tide—it comes in and it goes out.

Money isn't everything, but it's way ahead of the competition.

If poverty is a blessing in disguise, the disguise is perfect.

Money can't buy happiness—that's why we have credit cards.

Money can't buy happiness—but then happiness can't buy groceries.

My ambition is to be able to afford to spend what I'm spending.

If money talks, why isn't it doing some explaining.

Hush money is the proof that silence is golden.

 The best tranquilizer is money.

My financial problems are simple. I'm short on money.

Money talks, but it doesn't hear very well when you call it.

When it does talk, all my money says is "Goodbye."

Opportunity knocks only once, but not opportunists.

Poor? I could only have one measle at a time.

Every time I lose a dime it's my last one.

I've got enough money to last me a lifetime, unless I buy something.

For a shock treatment my psychiatrist sends his bills in advance.

I still remember my college days—all four of them.

I started school in the first grade. Years passed, but I didn't.

A snob is a guy who wears a riding habit to pitch horseshoes.

I sat on the bench so long I became very calloused.

It's a crime to catch a fish in some lakes, and a miracle in others.

The position I played on my college football team was drawback.

I don't ski. I'm headed downhill fast enough as it is.

What I enjoy most about table tennis is stepping on the ball.

He throws money around like a man without arms.

I'm not particular about how people treat me—just so long as they do.

The bulls and the bears aren't dangerous on Wall Street—it's the bum steers.

I've been burned in the stock market by picking up a hot tip.

Some stocks split—mine just crumble.

I only lack three things to get to the top: talent, ambition and initiative.

If hard work is the key to success, I'd rather pick the lock.

I don't mind the lies told about me, what worries me is the truth.

Who says nothing is impossible? I've been doing nothing for years.

CHAPTER 5
HEALTH/DIET

With all of today's attractive accident insurance policies, a man can't afford to die a natural death.

The only way you can get into a hospital quickly these days is by accident.

The air is about the only remaining thing that's free, and it's becoming dangerous to breathe.

The most frightening horror tales, are those told by bathroom scales.

This is a form fitting suit, unfortunately I don't have the form it fits.

I once boarded a boat and it became a submarine.

I'm so tense, my office furniture is overwrought iron.

More people commit suicide with a fork than with a gun.

The last thing a man wants to do is the last thing he does—die.

You can see by the obituary column that people die in alphabetical order.

 To diet you stop eating food and start eating calories.

I'm on a garlic diet. So far I've lost 5 pounds and 12 friends.

Dieting is the art of letting the hips fall where they may.

Diets are for people who are thick and tired of it.

The second day of a diet is easier than the first—by then you're off the diet.

Every time I go on a diet, the first thing I lose is my temper.

I went on a 14-day diet, but all I lost was two weeks.

After my medical exam I asked "Doc, how do I stand?" He said "That's what puzzles me."

It's double jeopardy when your doctor calls in a consultant.

Before treating my nose and ear, my doctor asked for an arm and leg.

I'm trying to find a doctor whose patients are not all sick.

I read about the evils of drinking, so I gave up reading.

Hangover: the wrath of grapes.

I do not drink like a fish. No fish drinks what I drink.

He's an outstanding candidate for the Alcohol of Fame.

Of all the remedies that won't cure a cold, I like whiskey the best.

I changed my mind, but it didn't work any better than my old one.

"Doctor, I have a ringing in my ear." "Don't answer it."

Carrots must be good for the eyes. You never see a rabbit wearing glasses.

Some people are born with black eyes—others have to fight for them.

A bright eye indicates curiosity; a black eye, too much curiosity.

I turned black and blue from overeating. I ate more than I could pay for.

The only thing digestible about a doughnut is the hole.

I've eaten so much sea food, my stomach rises and falls with the tide.

Indigestion is the failure to adjust a square meal to a round stomach.

A doughnut is a fried halo.

Hamburger is steak that didn't pass its physical.

Remember: a fly in the soup is better than no meat at all.

A barbecue often cooks steaks rare and fingers well done.

A hypochondriac can't leave being well-enough alone.

Some people call a doctor when all they want is an audience.

I don't know much about medicine, but I know what I like.

The fault I find with exercising is that it makes me tired.

A hypochondriac can suffer in many different ways, but never in silence.

I'm sure I've got the chicken pox—I found a feather in my bed.

 Hay fever is much achoo about nothing.

Hypochondria is a disease without a disease.

A manic-depressive is the easy glum, easy glow type.

I got out of a sick bed to get here—the bed is better.

I have a perfect cure for a sore throat—cut it.

What really happens if you exercise daily is that you die healthier.

Insanity is hereditary. You can get it from your children.

I've got a bad case of insomnia—I keep waking up every few days.

I walk in my sleep so I get my rest and my exercise at the same time.

I even get winded playing chess.

I do push-ups three times a day—from my chair, for meals.

Breathing is the secret of longevity—but only if you keep it up long enough.

A chronic complainer gets all his exercise out of kicking.

A man always loses weight when his wife is dieting.

Just once I'd like to be weighed and found wanting.

She had the mumps for two weeks before we noticed it.

The only thing about me that's getting thinner is my hair.

I once boarded a boat and it became a submarine.

I had to sign up for group insurance all by myself.

In my high school graduation picture, I was the front row.

I'm unable to contain myself.

Anything you say about me has to take in a lot of territory.

The way I eat it's no wonder I get thick to my stomach.

A stout person lives shorter, but eats longer.

The more you overeat, the harder it is to get close to the table.

I don't know much about medicine, but I know what I like.

My psychiatrist told me I was crazy. I said I wanted a second opinion. He said "O.K., you're ugly too!"

A psychiatric examination is a check up from the neck up.

I always step on my cigarette butts so they won't burn the rugs.

My wife gave up smoking but she keeps on fuming.

Smoke and the world smokes with you, quit and you smoke alone.

As ye smoke, so shall you reek.

What this country needs is a cigarette that will cure the smoking habit.

Many are cold, but few are chosen.

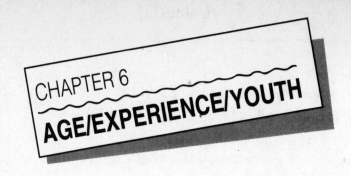

CHAPTER 6

AGE/EXPERIENCE/YOUTH

Adolescence is the awkward age in the life of a youngster. They're too old for an allowance and too young for a credit card.

A child is growing up when he stops asking where he comes from and starts refusing to tell you where he's going.

Adolescence is a period of rapid changes. Between the ages of twelve and seventeen, for example, a parent ages as much as twenty years.

Adults are really not wiser than children—they're just more cunning.

The best time to give your children advice is while they are still young enough to believe you know what you're talking about.

Old age is when you find yourself using one bend over to pick up two things.

Middle age is when a man is as young as he feels after trying to prove it.

A man has reached middle age when he is warned by a doctor to slow down instead of the police.

Life begins at forty—but you miss a lot of fun if you wait that long.

Adolescence is when you think you'll live forever. Middle age is when you wonder how you've lasted so long.

Maybe it's true that life begins at forty. But everything else starts to wear out, fall out or spread out.

You've reached the difficult age when you're too tired to work and too poor to quit.

One of the greatest pleasures of growing old is the freedom you enjoy from life insurance salesmen.

The reason some people become old before their time is because they had a time before they got old.

Middle age is when you get enough exercise just avoiding people who think you should have more.

Middle age has set in when you become exhausted by your teenager telling you how he spent an evening.

It requires a great deal of inexperience to be beyond the reach of anxiety.

You're getting old when you spend more talking to your druggist than you do to your bartender.

Forget my birthday. It's much kinder not to send me a reminder.

I have a clean conscience, because I've never used it.

Conscience is a thing that feels terrible when everything else feels great.

The good die young because only the young die good.

He looks as if an undertaker started on him and was called away.

I was the teacher's pet. She couldn't afford a dog.

Wisdom often comes with age, but with him age came alone.

My wife bought a cheap dictionary—its not in alphabetical order.

The trouble with experience is that so few of us are born with it.

I lost my glasses and can't look for them until I find them.

My golf is improving. Yesterday I hit the ball in one.

I never tell a lie—if the truth will do more damage.

As long as you can count your gray hairs, they don't count.

Another form of endurance test is the pursuit of happiness.

He isn't bald; he just has a tall face.

What good is happiness? It can't buy you money.

Show me a wrinkle, and I'll show you the nick of time.

Insomnia is the triumph of mind over mattress.

To avoid having enemies, outlive them.

Very few people have the courage of my convictions.

It's a wise crack that knows its own father.

I'm fast on the ad-lib. All I have to do is hear it once.

I hope to live to be as old as my jokes.

Today's accent is on youth—but the stress is on the parents.

Imagine a kid so rotten, he's got a scholarship to reform school.

To this day, I still chase women—but only if it's downhill.

In my neighborhood the kids used barbed wire for dental floss.

Talk about a tough kid. All his tattooing is done by a stone mason.

Knowledge is power—if you know it about the right people.

Living it up is always a prelude to trying to live it down.

An autobiography is the story of how a man thinks he lived.

For every man over sixty five there are seven women—but by then it's too late.

This I believe—nothing risque, nothing gained.

I once dislocated both shoulders describing a fish I caught.

Children learn to lie by watching adults who pretend they don't.

Opportunities lie at every hand, and so do a lot of people.

Lately I burn the midnight oil about 9:00 p.m.

I've given up exercising—pushing fifty is enough exercise for me.

I'm beginning to think that my gray hair isn't premature.

Of course I'm against sin—I'm against anything I'm too old to enjoy.

 Old age is an incurable disease.

To this day, I still chase women—but only if it's downhill.

Calling a man a "sexagenarian" sounds like flattery.

In youth we pursue physical culture—in age, fiscal fitness.

I don't have to learn history—I remember it.

I'd retire rich if I could sell my experience for what it cost me.

Spring may be in the air, but it's not in me.

The old maid sighed when she died, "Who said you can't take it with you?"

I never do anyone harm—unless I can do myself good.

September is the month when most little boys develop class hatred.

The kids in my class were so tough, the teacher played hookey.

Before you retire, take a week off and watch daytime television.

An alarm clock is a non-alcoholic eye opener.

When I looked at my passport photo I realized I needed the trip.

You can't take it with you, but don't try to travel without it.

I can make it rain anytime. All I do is wash my car.

I was born in the winter, a penguin brought me instead of a stork.

CHAPTER 7
WORK/PROFESSIONS

Show me an archaeologist, and I'll show you a man who practices skullduggery.

Anybody who thinks talk is cheap hasn't argued with a traffic cop.

If all your barber does is talk your ear off, you've got plenty to be thankful for.

A good barber and a good tailor can take years off a man's life—but you can't fool a flight of stairs.

The only man who is never criticized when he lies down on the job is a blood donor.

Business is so quiet you can hear the overhead piling up.

When crime stops paying, gangsters and politicians will do something else.

I learned to steal so that I could follow in my father's fingerprints.

If crime doesn't pay, how come it's one of the biggest businesses?

A successful burglar can afford to stop making house calls.

Crime doesn't pay, but at least you are your own boss.

Critic: one who is quick on the flaw.

My sister dated an undertaker, but he just wanted her body.

My son is a born doctor. He can't write anything anybody can read.

A specialist is a doctor with a smaller practice, but a larger income.

Doctors should let the well enough alone.

The only doctor who never sends his patients a bill is the veterinarian.

My doctor says I need a complete change—so I'm changing my doctor.

My doctor is so busy, while in his waiting room I caught another disease.

My doctor is mean. He keeps his stethoscope in the freezer.

My doctor's prescriptions are hard to read, but his bills are legible.

He may not look it, but he's a police dog. You see, he's in the C.I.A.

My brother wanted to be a lawyer badly, but he became a bad lawyer.

I know of a jack-of-all-trades who is out of work in all of them.

 I finally started selling furniture for a living—my own.

I'm very responsible. No matter what goes wrong—I'm responsible.

I'm going to learn a trade—so that I'll know what kind of work I'm out of.

As an inducement to hard work nothing beats a big family.

I try not to have coffee in the morning. It keeps me awake all day.

The reason pediatricians eat so well is that children don't.

My barber says my hair is getting thin. So who wants fat hair.

He who eats an apple a day is frowned about by the A.M.A.

I've done some screen work—I fixed one on our kitchen door.

One traveling salesman died and left his family 5,000 hotel towels.

If bankers can count, why do they always have eight windows and two tellers.

The reason Robin Hood robbed the rich was because the poor had no money.

A comic is a person, who, when he dies, is at his wits end.

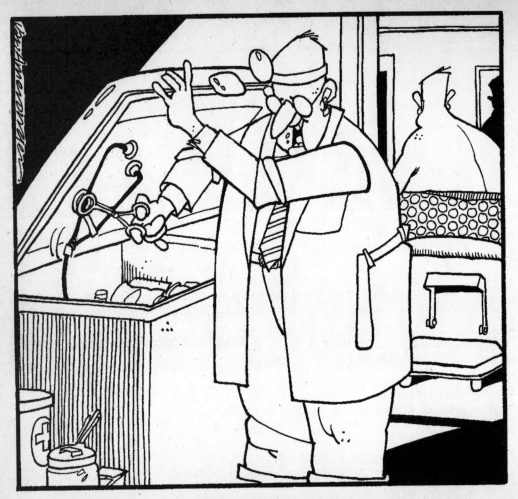

My doctor is mean. He keeps his stethoscope in the freezer.

I wrote my own gags to keep the wolf from the door. I told them to the wolf.

He had a defect, which to a comic might be fatal. He wasn't funny.

A gag writer is a person who has hitched his gaggin' to a star.

In literature it is the satirist who rules with an irony hand.

Some comedians couldn't cheer up a laughing hyena.

Is he funny? He appears once and suffers from over-exposure.

A comic is a man who makes dough out of corn.

A comic is a man who originates old jokes.

A poet has a great imagination; he imagines people will read his poetry.

My agent gets 10% of everything I get, except my blinding headaches.

Lawyers sometimes tell the truth—they'll do anything to win a case.

Anyone can sit on a jury, but it takes a lawyer to sit on a witness.

My lawyer was hurt—the ambulance backed up suddenly.

Suppression is nine points of the law.

Divorces are arranged so lawyers can live happily ever after.

A lawyer is a person who helps you get what's coming to him.

You can't live with lawyers and you can't die without them.

It takes a lot of suits to keep a lawyer well dressed.

A law firm is successful when it has more clients than partners.

Ignorance of the law excuses no man—from practicing it.

A lawyer is a man who profits by your experience.

The truly successful lawyer owns his own ambulance.

Hard work never killed anyone—neither did not working.

If I were any steadier as a worker I'd be motionless.

I'm not afraid of hard work—I've fought it successfully for years.

My boss's son has a malady that malingers on.

I like to have my work cut out for me entirely.

In December I worked my fingers to the bonus.

I joined six unions to be sure of always being out on strike.

Even if his ship would come in, he wouldn't bother to unload it.

I had to pay $25.00 to get my library card back. I didn't return the librarian for two weeks.

I know a microscope expert—he magnifies everything.

I guess a monumental liar is a guy who writes epitaphs.

In a psychiatrist's office you lie on a couch to tell the truth.

My boss has a testimonial plaque from Simon Legree.

My boss is always unpleasant, even when you catch him off guard.

I'll never forget my first words in the theater. "Peanuts, Popcorn!"

Incognito in Hollywood means: "I wish someone would recognize me."

Most film actors can't stand success—especially if it's someone else's.

In Hollywood, you're a genius until you lose your job.

They shot the film in a hurry—previewed it, and then shot the director.

Good musicians execute their music—bad ones murder it.

Some performers take pains with their music, others give them.

Banjo players get $50.00 per hour. That's pretty easy picking.

Psychiatrist's ad: "Two couches—no waiting."

My analyst is an ambivalence chaser.

 In Ireland psychiatrists use Murphy beds.

My analyst is so busy he has an upper and lower berth.

College professors get what's left after the football coach is paid.

I held the audience opened mouth—they all yawned at the same time.

Ad in Variety: "Lion-Tamer, looking for tamer lion."

A boxer is a fellow who wakes up and finds himself rich.

A pugilist is a boxer with an education.

It takes a sports expert to write the best alibis for being wrong.

A basketball player is a guy interested in plugging loop holes.

He was a colorful fighter—black and blue all over.

A broker is seldom original, but great with quotations.

A broker is a man who runs your fortune into a shoestring.

No man goes before his time—unless his boss has left early.

The reason I work so hard is that I'm too nervous to steal.

Our housekeeper's idea of work is to sweep the room with a glance.

An assistant is a fellow who can't get off.

I've handled some pretty big jobs, I used to house-break elephants.

Work is all right if it doesn't take up too much of your spare time.

I may get to work late, but I make up for it by leaving early.

It takes me an hour to get to work—after I get there.

Hard work never hurt anyone who hired someone else to do it.

I work like a horse, but only when my boss rides me.

Work is good for you—it's labor that kills.

My greatest pleasure in life is having lots to do, and not doing it.

Like every man of sense and good feeling, I hate work.

CHAPTER 8
THE SEXES

Eve was the first person who ate herself out of house and home.

Writing is the only respectable profession where a woman can do her work in bed.

The reason men like blondes is because they get dirty quicker.

I got a real kick out of kissing her. Her husband caught me.

I want a girl, just like the girl, that Dad had on the side.

My word is as good as my blonde.

A good girl is good but a bad girl is better.

This place is so old fashioned, the couples were dancing together.

My neighbors couldn't afford a divorce, so she shot him.

Divorce is the result of compatibility turning into combatibility.

I know a surgeon who takes out tonsils, appendixes, and nurses.

Everything about her is open—an open mind with a vacant stare.

A polite man offers a lady a seat when he gets off the bus.

All the world loves a lover—except her husband.

Then I ordered dinner for a party of eighteen—and, could she eat!

I never expect to find the perfect girl—but it's been great fun searching.

In a beauty parlor, the gossip alone can curl your hair.

All her gray matter is outside her head.

 Birth control is the evasion of the issue.

A little honey is good for you—unless your wife finds out.

I take so many different colored pills, I dream in Technicolor.

A Hollywood triangle is made up of an actor, his wife and himself.

The Sexes

~~~~~~

"I'm interested in the sport of kings." "Horses?" "No, queens."

To sell something, tell a woman it's a bargain; tell a man it's deductible.

Wine, women and song ruined me. I didn't get any.

Some women show their sense of humor by their choice of husband.

His marriage was a mistake—his wife's.

I've kissed so many women I can do it with my eyes closed.

Some men court, then marry, then go to court again.

It's better to have loved and lost—yeah, lots better.

~~~~~~

I got a real kick out of kissing her. Her husband caught me.

A love story is a comedy of Eros.

Platonic love is like being invited into a bar to sample the water.

When a man loses his heart, his head has to do double the work.

The man who loses his heart usually loses his head as well.

Lover's lane is a secluded place with indoor-outdoor car-petting.

Every woman marries for love, even if it's only love of money.

If my love affair was on television—I'd change channels.

Love is blind. That's why I use the touch system.

It used to be love at first sight; now it's love at every opportunity.

I usually treat a woman to rum and coax.

Love is propaganda for propagation.

In college, I signed up for all the romance languages.

I never pass up a chance to mix business with pleasure.

All I know about women is what I pick up.

I have two hobbies: collecting old masters and young mistresses.

The current trend is towards shorter honeymoons, but more of them.

Marriage is the billing after the cooing.

A perfect man is a wife's first husband.

There's nothing like a wedding to bring two married people together.

The secret of a happy marriage: Don't go to bed angry—stay up and fight.

It's not who you know that's important—it's how your wife found out.

How can they outlaw gambling as long as marriage is legal?

The worst part about a second marriage is breaking in a new mother-in-law.

In a nudist camp you learn that not all men are created equal.

You're getting old when all girls look alike to you.

I'm looking for a rich girl who's too proud to have her husband work.

I'm not troubled by sexual fantasies—in fact, I rather enjoy them.

I used to date a teacher who didn't have a principle.

A woman with a past attracks men who hope history will repeat itself.

A brainless beauty is a toy forever.

The man who can read women like a book usually likes to read in bed.

These days a girl is known by the company that keeps her.

Sex is the poor man's polo.

In the war of the sexes, there are no conscientious objectors.

Sex proves that it is easier to get two bodies together than two souls.

An extramarital affair is often a game not worth the scandal.

The only unnatural sex act is that which you cannot perform.

One reason sex is so popular is that it's centrally located.

Some girls go in for swimming, while others know every dive.

Many a girl thinks she is fond of sports until she marries one.

A cheap date is a guy who walks you to a drive-in.

I learned French is six easy liaisons.

I should have known how jealous my wife is—she had male bridesmaids.

She can bring more bills into the house than Congress.

CHAPTER 9

AMERICAN LIFE/
GOVERNMENT/TAXES

Before pollution people used to get air sick only on planes.

Americans are an idealistic people, and we'll make any sacrifice for a cause so long as it won't hurt business.

People in foreign countries are not really rude; they're just trying to imitate Americans.

I see where several of our politicians are predicting a return of prosperity as soon as business picks up.

The penalty for cheating is the disgrace of dying rich.

I'm a very highly suspected person in my community.

Santa's elves have organized. They call their union the A.F. of Elves.

This town has some of the best cops money can buy.

We can't seem to stop crime—so let's legalize it and tax it out of business.

The difficulty is not buying on time—it's paying on time.

Some dogs are pointers. Mine's a nudger. He's too polite to point.

The perfect dog food would be one that tastes like a postal carrier.

When you go in a restaurant always ask for a table near a waiter.

Sign at bar: If you're drinking to forget, please pay in advance.

I never shot billiards—they have as much right to live as anyone else.

His brain is like a politician's speech—mostly empty.

Chicago is so windy that it's possible to spit in your own eye.

Once, large families were the rule, not the exemptions.

When you go in a restaurant always ask for a table near a waiter.

In the armed forces, mess call is the battle cry of feed 'em.

A typical American snack is pizza, chow mein, and blintzes.

You can't beat the climate in Las Vegas—or the slot machines.

Las Vegas isn't a city—it's a garbage disposal for money.

Las Vegas has two main sources of income: seven and eleven.

Las Vegas is always crowded because no one has the fare to leave.

My lawyer says that where there's a will, there's an ill.

A hospital is a place where they wake you up to give you a sleeping pill.

A modern miracle would be a diamond wedding anniversary in Hollywood.

A lot of politicians give publicly and steal privately.

The field of humor is crowded when Congress is in session.

Diplomacy is the art of lying in state.

Horses are what more people bet on than get on.

In pitching horseshoes the first rule is to remove the horse.

The race track is a place where windows clean people.

My horse was so slow they paid the jockey time-and-a-half for overtime.

The best way to stop a runaway horse is to bet on it.

If 50,000 people ran at a race track, not one horse would attend.

I think the name of my hotel is "The Outstretched Palms."

My hotel is so dull, last night I sent down for another bible.

They change the sheets daily—from one room to another.

My hotel is very big. To call the desk you dial long distance.

Remember "motel" spelled backwards is "let 'em."

Business is so bad, some hotels are stealing towels from the guests.

The field of humor is crowded when Congress is in session.

Income is a small matter to me—especially after taxes.

Maybe we can keep warm next winter by burning our bills.

Maybe we can keep warm next winter by burning our bills.

Inflation affects everything—including the wages of sin.

At today's prices you're lucky if you can make one end meet.

Once price indicated value, now it's an indication of nerve.

 If prices are coming down, they all have parachutes.

Inflation is when the money you haven't got is worth less than before.

Today, of you're not confused, you're not well-informed.

My lawyer once got the jury so confused, they sent the judge to jail.

When judge and jury are against the defendant, 13 is an unlucky number.

Judges without convictions are the most generous in handing them out.

It takes a thief to catch a thief, and a jury to let him go.

Life is made up of trials, appeals, reversals, but few convictions.

Life is like an artichoke—you go through so much to get so little.

Man is illogical—he wishes for a long life but never for old age.

All you can get for a dollar today is change.

If you think today's dollar doesn't go far, try to get one back.

Poverty is no disgrace, but that's all one can say in it's favor.

I'm in favor of capital punishment; capital deserves it.

Hard cash is the softest thing to fall back on.

The happy ending in many films is the fact the picture has ended.

The films we slept through in theaters, now keep us awake on TV.

We throw flowers at the dead, and mud at the living.

I thought I was intelligent until I was tried by a jury of my peers.

Nudists suffer from clothes-trophobia.

I could never be a nudist. I always spill hot coffee in my lap.

Today, if you're not confused, you're not well-informed.

Where does a nudist put his keys after he locks the car?

Some nudists won't even ask for dressing on their salad.

The principal cause of insanity is indictments.

In Hollywood, if you don't have an analyst people think you're crazy.

Without basketball, where would high school dances be held?

Some of the most insecure things in the world are called "securities."

People who play the market are often led astray by false profits.

There's many a slip between the stock and the tip.

I'm doing well in the market this week—my broker is on vacation.

I made a killing in the Stock Market. I shot my broker.

A taxpayer is a person who has the government on his payroll.

After paying my taxes I feel that all my success I owe to Uncle Sam.

The Tax Collector is looking for untold wealth.

Any man who doesn't complain about taxes is either very rich or very poor.

The I.R.S. must love poor people—it's creating so many of them.

It's hard to believe that America was founded to avoid taxes.

In pitching horseshoes the first rule is to remove the horse.

I have no trouble filing my income tax—but I have trouble paying.

I just send my income to Washington—who can afford taxes.

A dime is a dollar with all the taxes taken out.

Congress passes bills—the taxpayers pay them.

A tax cut is the kindest cut of all.

Save your pennies—the dollars go to the I.R.S.

If crime could be taxed, there would be no need for other taxes.

The I.R.S. not only believes what it is told, but twice as much.

Taxation without representation was tyranny, but it was a lot cheaper.

The income tax form is the only blank that's loaded.

Taxes are a form of Capitol punishment.

On television the happy ending is always preceded by a bad commercial.

We now interrupt the commercial to bring you a television program.

Television is where old movies go to die.

TV commercials wouldn't be so bad if they weren't so often.

Television is where the law of the jingle prevails.

"The good die young" does not refer to television jokes.

I was never on television, but I was on radar twice on the Freeway.

We all have to go sometime—usually during commercials.

The good things on television last night were the vase and the clock.

Television's biggest problem is killing time between commercials.

Television is the greatest aid to sleep since darkness.

The English drive on the left side of the road—just like in California.

Sign in a travel agent's window: Why don't you go away?

Rain makes the flowers grow, and the taxis disappear.

CHAPTER 10

HUMAN NATURE

After you've heard two eyewitness accounts of an auto accident, you begin to worry about history.

One good thing about apathy is you don't have to exert yourself to show you're sincere about it.

A bartender is the only psychiatrist who never tells anyone to give up drinking.

Happiness is getting a bill you've already paid, so you can sit down and write a nasty letter.

I'm very superstitious. In a fight, I always keep a horseshoe in my glove.

Human Nature

If you think it's easy to take candy away from a baby—you should try it.

Why does Christmas always come when the stores are so crowded.

Seen the price of Christmas trees? This year the tree trimmed me.

Christmas Eve is the night that Santa keeps his ho's to the grindstone.

Are Santa's helpers known as subordinate clauses?

Anyone with a clear conscience probably has a bad memory.

Some men take two hours to tell you why they are a man of few words.

Repartee is what you think of on the way home.

He's so crooked he'd steal two left shoes.

The wages of sin are the high cost of low living.

Poverty isn't a crime, but it counts against you if you commit one.

Criticism wouldn't be so hard to take if it weren't so often right.

Everybody wants to go to heaven, but nobody wants to die.

Dead men tell no tales, but their obituaries often do.

Always borrow from a pessimist—he never expects it back.

You're drunk when you feel sophisticated and can't pronounce it.

Laugh and the world laughs with you. Cry and they say you're drunk.

A drunk put a dime in a parking meter and said "My God—I weigh an hour!"

When two egotists meet, it's a case of an I for an I.

If his halo falls one more inch, it will be a noose.

He's carrying on a great love affair—unassisted.

His dream is to go from the cash register to the social register.

It's not true that vanity is a sin. Sometimes it's a mistake.

The course of true love never runs smooth, except when it's self-love.

A gentleman is one who never insults anyone intentionally.

If you don't go to a friend's funeral, don't expect him to come to your's.

Cultivate good manners, and you'll be mistaken for a doorman.

Never add cream and sugar to your coffee after it's in the saucer.

Some people have tact—others tell the truth.

A well-bred man steps on his cigarette before it can burn a hole in the carpet.

For years I ate with the wrong fingers.

Once you taste English coffee, you know why they drink tea.

I almost went blind drinking coffee—I left the spoon in the cup.

A man's best friend is his dog, and his worst enemy is his dogma.

I have property in Las Vegas. Caesar's Palace has my luggage.

I'll let anybody borrow my lawn mower as long as they keep it in my yard.

If you don't grow your own vegetables, praise your neighbor's garden.

What mother used to call "sin," daughter now calls "experience."

In golf, the ball always lies poorly; and the player well.

Golf is about the only thing that depreciates above par.

The course of true golf never did run smooth.

I never put off till tomorrow the gossip I can spread today.

A gossip listens in haste and repeats at leisure.

I never repeat gossip, so listen carefully the first time.

A gossip burns her scandals at both ends.

An operation is a surgical job taking minutes to do and years to describe.

Honesty is the best policy, but many are satisfied with less than the best.

Honesty pays—and dishonest gets paid.

Human Nature

An honest confession is good for the soul, but bad for the reputation.

I never go back on my word—without consulting my lawyer.

At least an introvert spends his time minding his own business.

Behavior patterns are trait jackets.

Nobody ever knows a poet is alive until he is dead.

A joke is a form of humor enjoyed by some and misunderstood by most.

A bad joke is like a bad egg—all the worse for having been cracked.

Old jokes never die, they just sound that way.

I have property in Las Vegas. Caesar's Palace has my luggage.

Human Nature

Truth is stranger than fiction, and also harder to make up.

Supply and demand sets prices. You pay what the store demands.

If a little learning is a dangerous thing, then most people are safe.

An intelligent man knows everything, a shrewd man knows everybody.

When there's a will there's a law suit.

A witness has to swear to tell the truth before he starts to lie.

Honesty is the best policy, because good lawyers are expensive.

Some people are so lazy they get in a revolving door and wait.

Even his car is shiftless.

Pity the poor kleptomaniac who found himself in a piano store.

If you can't love your enemies, compromise: forget them.

Be careful when you stretch the truth too far—it may snap back.

The man who says he never tells lies is telling one.

Most fish would be bigger if fishermen's arms were longer.

 Actions lie louder than words.

The big advantage of being truthful is that your lies are believed.

Human Nature

Some people love the truth, and some hate to get caught in a lie.

One thing an alarm clock never arouses in me is my better nature.

Talk about disagreeable, his own shadow won't keep him company.

I may not be disgruntled, but I'm certainly far from being gruntled.

A grouch is a man who spreads good cheer wherever he doesn't go.

A successful man is one who can earn more than his family can spend.

Money constantly changes hands—and people.

A fool and his money—are invited places.

A wealthy playboy is a "Cashanova."

Money is what you swap for what you think will make you happy.

Many people are unprejudiced—by the facts.

When an opportunist lays his cards on the table—count them.

The only time to deal with him is when he isn't himself.

I started as an unwanted child, but now I'm wanted in seven states.

An opportunist always tries to land on someone else's feet.

An optimist believes that a fly is looking for a way to get out.

Human Nature

Guy to psychiatrist, "Nobody talks to me." Psychiatrist says, "Next."

A school is a mental institution.

Education enables you to get into more expensive trouble.

Only the wages of sin have no deductions.

Two things never live up to their advertising claims: the circus and sin.

Of two sins, choose the one you enjoy the most.

There may be no rest for the wicked, but there is often arrest.

All work and no plagiarism makes a dull speech.

Maybe a fish goes home and lies about the size of the bait he stole.

To catch a fish you have to worm your way into its confidence.

The way he avoids picking up a check—you have to hand it to him.

There are no atheists in the waiting room of the I.R.S.

Every time I ask what time it is I get a different answer.

Truth is merely a lazy expedient of the imagination.

It was so cold, we even welcomed a hotfoot.

Cold? My color television turned blue.

I can't understand why it's still raining—the weekend is over.

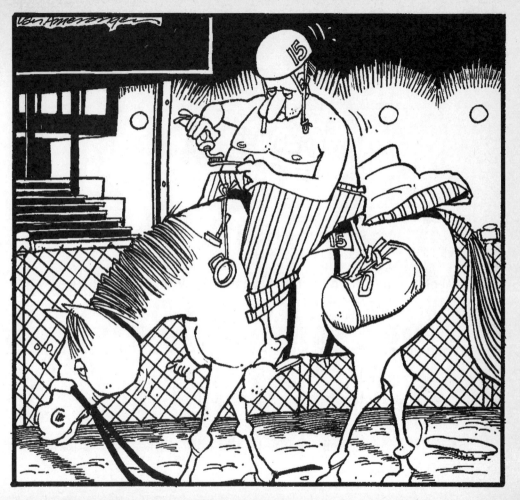

My horse came in so late the jockey was wearing pajamas.

CHAPTER 11
PEOPLE

Did you hear about the Southern bigot who was a bed wetter? He used to go to Klan meetings in a rubber sheet.

When I meet a man of convictions I wonder how many he has served time for.

When all is said and done, some people just keep on talking.

A man with a reputation for being energetic may merely be nervous.

The closest some people come to a brainstorm is a light drizzle.

People

~~~~~~

He was born stupid, and lately he's had a relapse.

He's brighter than he looks—but then, he'd just have to be.

If he ever gets a bright idea it'll be beginner's luck.

He's afraid to be lost in thought—he's a total stranger there.

He's so dumb, the mind reader only charged him half price.

She's recovering from an accident—a thought recently struck her.

What you don't know doesn't hurt you, but it amuses a lot of people.

He has the manners of a gentleman. I knew they didn't belong to him.

~~~~~~

Some people sleep with one eye open; others are awake with both eyes shut.

You can always count on him to hit the nail squarely on the thumb.

The ideal way to serve leftovers is to somebody else.

The last time I had a hot meal was when a candle fell in my TV dinner.

I have no enemies—all my friends hate me.

He hasn't an enemy in the world and none of his friends like him.

I had a really fine friend—he stabbed me in the front.

When I play bridge is when I get good poker hands.

People

Always sympathize with the underdog, but never bet on him.

I detest gossip—but only when it's about me.

My handicap, in golf, is honesty.

My horse came in so late the jockey was wearing pajamas.

The hotel bath towels are so fluffy you can hardly close your suitcase.

No two people are alike and both of them are glad of it.

I would trust other people more if I knew myself less.

Why does a hostess insist on introducing us to people we don't know.

Today people don't repent—even at leisure.

 He who laughs last, doesn't get the joke.

Nothing annoys me more than a man who thinks he know it all and does.

Some people stop to think and then forget to start again.

If you know all the answers, you probably misunderstood the question.

The man who thinks he knows everything irritates those of us who do.

I like the parable about the multitude that loafs and fishes.

Even his nose is lazy. It won't even run when he has a cold.

Lazy! He wouldn't even help his mother-in-law move out of his house.

I'm going to the dogs faster than a flea.

I'm counting on a reduction in the wages of sin.

You can't believe some people, even when they swear they are lying.

Truth may not be stranger than fiction, but it's scarcer.

Some people can't even tell the truth in a diary.

Some people take the bull by the horns—I shoot it.

I'm a second story man. No one ever believes my first story.

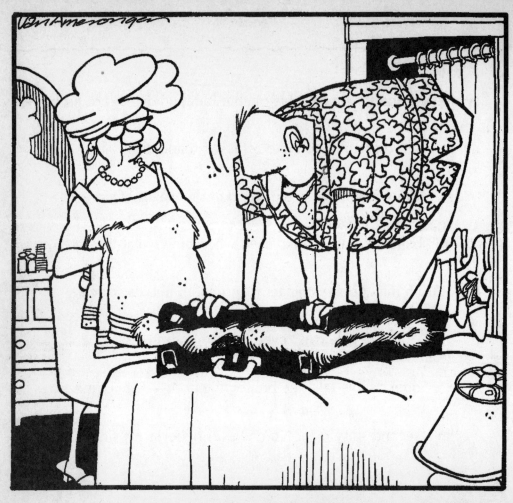

The hotel bath towels are so fluffy you can hardly close your suitcase.

People

At a party, I'm the guy who always starts the bull rolling.

I don't really exaggerate—I just remember big.

I've never been known to burn the candor at both ends.

You can believe half of what he tells you—the question is: which half?

Half the lies they tell about me are not true.

If I smile when things go wrong, it means I have someone around to blame it on.

I had three phones installed, so I can hang up on more people.

I had such a long face, the barber charged me double for a shave.

Always keep your words soft and sweet—one day you may have to eat them.

Some people pay you a compliment like they expect a receipt.

I don't mind criticism just so long as it is unqualified praise.

I won't be contented with my lot until it's a lot more.

Never hit a man when he's down—he might get up again.

People who have a lot to say shouldn't go to a concert to say it.

A quartet is four people who think the other three can't sing.

A musical ignoramus is one who doesn't know his brass from his oboe.

People

Singing in the bathtub is called a "soap opera."

Music hath charms to soothe a savage beast—but I'd try a rifle first.

An opportunist remembers what he gives and forgets what he gets.

An opportunist will always help you get what's coming to him.

Give an opportunist a free hand and he'll stick it right in your pocket.

An opportunist is always ready to back his hot tips with your cash.

I didn't really dislike school. It was the principal of the thing.

Many people buy on time, but only a few pay that way.

He only picks up the check if it's made out to him.

The only thing he ever gave away was a secret.

He's so tight, he even refuses to perspire freely.

He's a man of rare gifts—it's rare when he gives one.

I'm a man who gives no quarter—any waiter can testify to that.

Our flight was so rough, they poured the food directly into the airsick bags.